WALES

WORLD ADVENTURES

BY HARRIET BRUNDLE

BookLife

©2017
Book Life
King's Lynn
Norfolk PE30 4LS

ISBN: 978-1-78637-152-2

Written by:
Harriet Bundle

Edited by:
Charlie Ogden

Designed by:
Evie Wright

A catalogue record for this book
is available from the British Library.

WALES
WORLD ADVENTURES

CONTENTS

Words in **red** can be found in the glossary on page 24.

WHERE IS WALES?

The United Kingdom is a country in Europe.
It is made up of four smaller countries called England,
Scotland, Wales and Northern Ireland.

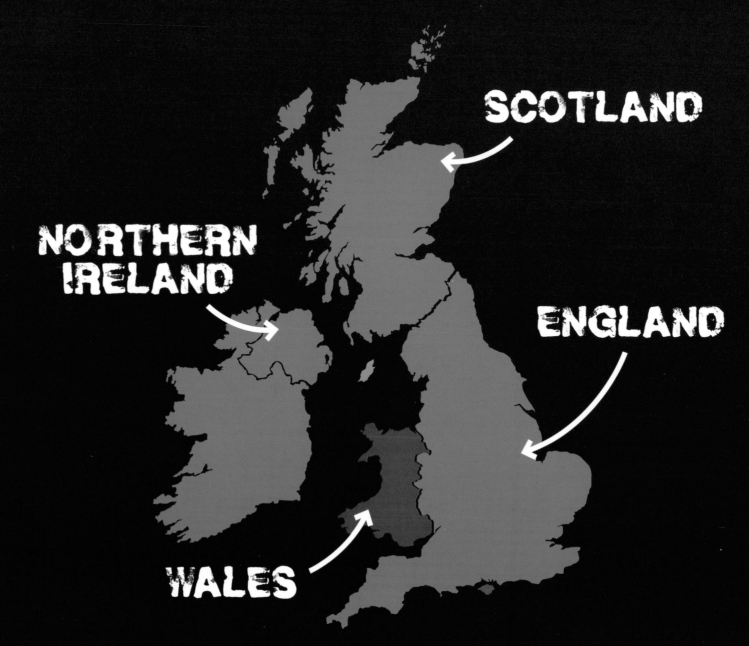

SCOTLAND

NORTHERN
IRELAND

ENGLAND

WALES

The **population** of Wales is over three million. The two main languages spoken in Wales are English and Welsh.

The capital city of Wales is Cardiff.

THE WELSH FLAG

WEATHER AND LANDSCAPE

The weather in Wales changes with the **seasons**. It is often warm in the summer and cold in the winter.

Wales has lots of different **landscapes.** There are beaches and mountains as well as lakes and rivers in the countryside.

Many people enjoy going on holiday to Wales.

BALA LAKE, WALES

CLOTHING

Welsh people usually wear **modern**, comfortable clothing. In the summer, people often wear shorts and t-shirts.

SHAWL

It is **traditional** for women in Wales to wear a shawl with a black hat. Today, this is often worn during **festivals**.

RELIGION

The **religion** with the most followers in Wales is Christianity. A Christian place of **worship** is called a church.

Some people in Wales follow the religion of Islam. People who follow Islam are called Muslims.

Many people in Wales do not follow any religion.

FOOD

CAWL

Cawl is a popular meal in Wales. Cawl is a soup that is usually made with meat, potatoes and vegetables.

Welsh cakes are a traditional snack in Wales. Welsh cakes are usually round in shape and can be eaten hot or cold.

WELSH CAKES

AT SCHOOL

Children in Wales start going to school when they are 5 years old and they usually finish when they are 18 years old.

Children in Wales are taught how to speak Welsh at school.

Lots of children in Wales enjoy going to after-school clubs.

AT HOME

Many people in Wales live in busy cities. In cities there are lots of houses, restaurants and shops.

CARDIFF, WALES

In **rural** parts of Wales there are lots of old buildings, such as castles. The houses in rural Wales are often made out of stone.

CONWY CASTLE, WALES

FAMILIES

In Wales, many children live with their parents, brothers and sisters.

Every family is different!

Lots of people in Wales also live near to other family members, such as their grandparents, aunts and uncles.

Families often get together to celebrate birthdays and festivals.

SPORT

One of the most popular sports in Wales is rugby. People in Wales started playing rugby around 150 years ago.

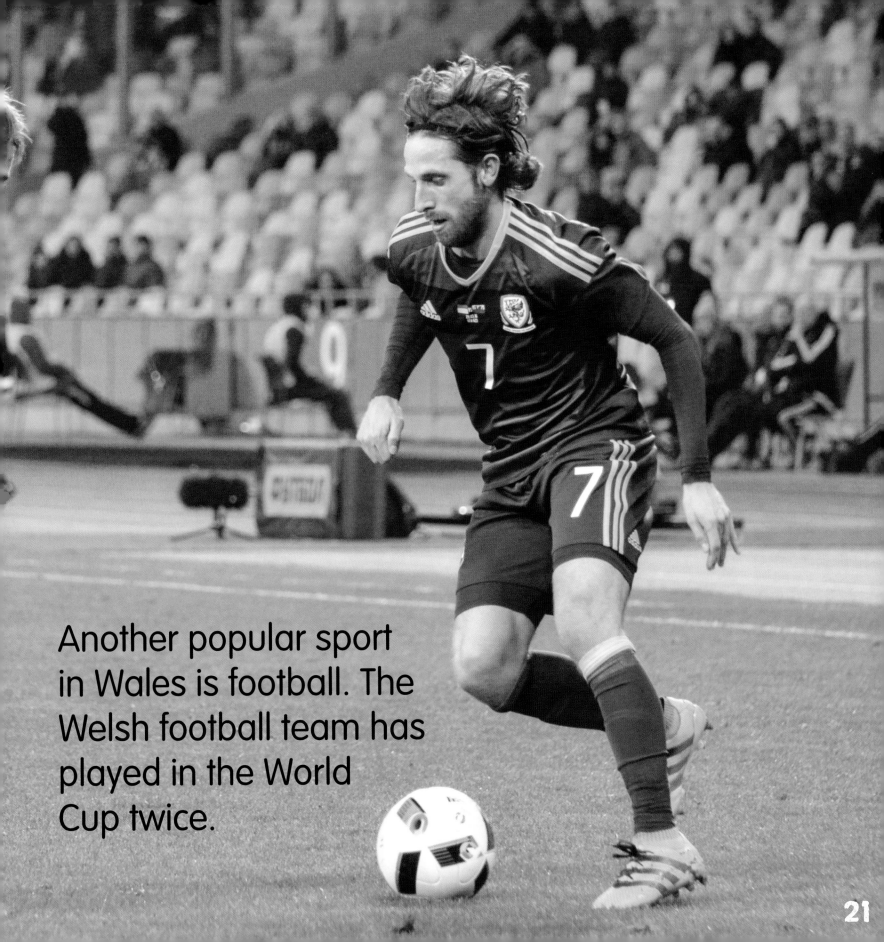

Another popular sport in Wales is football. The Welsh football team has played in the World Cup twice.

FUN FACTS

Roald Dahl was born in South Wales in 1916. He wrote Charlie and the Chocolate Factory and The BFG.

There are three sheep for every one person in Wales.

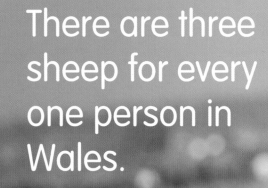

Cockles are often served with bacon for breakfast in Wales.

The red dragon has been a symbol of Wales for over 1,000 years.

GLOSSARY

Europe a large area of land that is made up of many countries

festivals times when people come together to celebrate special events

landscapes the visible features of areas of land

modern from recent or present times

population number of people living in a place

religion the belief in and worship of a god or gods

rural relating to the countryside

seasons the four periods of the year; spring, summer, autumn and winter

traditional related to very old behaviours or beliefs

worship a religious act such as praying

INDEX

Photocredits: Abbreviations: l-left, r-right, b-bottom, t-top, c-centre, m-middle. All images are courtesy of Shutterstock.com.

Front Cover – Petch One. 2 – ED Reardon. 3 – Valua Vitaly. 5 – Billy Stock. 6 – Eddie Cloud. 7 – Steve Meese. 8 – Tomsickova Tatayana. 9 – Anton Ivanov. 10 – Spumador. 11 – Lissma. 12 – Fanfo. 13 – Neil Langan. 14 – Luminast. 15 – Pressmaster. 16 – Philip Bird LRPS CPAGB. 17 – Samot. 17r – Milosz Maslanka. 18 – Halfpoint. 19 – Monkey Business Images. 20 – Paolo Bono. 21 – Vlad1988. 22 – Carl Van Vechten. 23 – Tcareob72. 23r - Jane McIlroy.
With thanks to Getty Images, Thinkstock Photo and iStockphoto.